21ST
CENTURY
DEBATES

KT-572-694

AN OVERCROWDED WORLD?

OUR IMPACT ON THE PLANET

ROB BOWDEN

University of Worcester
ILS Peirson Building
Henwick Grove, Worcester WR2 6AJ

W
HODDER
Wayland

an imprint of Hodder Children's Books

A1058881

21st Century Debates Series

Air Pollution • Endangered Species • Energy • Climate Change • Food Supply • Genetics • Internet • Media •
An Overcrowded World? • Rainforests • Surveillance • Waste, Recycling and Reuse • Artificial Intelligence •
Water Supply • World Health • Global Debt • Terrorism • The Drugs Trade • Racism • Violence in Society •
Transport and the Environment • Tourism • New Religious Movements • Globalisation

Produced for Hodder Wayland by White-Thomson Publishing Ltd,
2/3 St Andrew's Place, Lewes, East Sussex BN7 1UP

School
Resource
Area

University of Worcester
Library

A 1058881

363.9 BOW

© 2002 White-Thomson Publishing Ltd

Published in Great Britain in 2002 by Hodder Wayland, an imprint of Hodder Children's Books
This paperback edition published in 2003

Project editor: Kelly Davis
Commissioning editor: Steve White-Thomson
Proofreader: David C. Sills, Proof Positive Reading Service
Series and book design: Chris Halls, Mind's Eye Design
Picture research: Shelley Noronha, Glass Onion Pictures

All rights reserved. No part of this publication may be reproduced, stored in a retrieval system, or transmitted, in any
form or by any means without the prior written permission of the publisher, nor be otherwise circulated in any form
of binding or cover other than that in which it is published and without a similar condition being imposed on the
subsequent purchaser.

British Cataloguing in Publication Data
Bowden, Rob
  An overcrowded world?. - (21st century debates)
  1. Population - Juvenile literature
  I. Title
  363.9
ISBN 0 7502 4455 0

Printed and bound in Italy by G. Canale & C.S.p.A., Turin

Hodder Children's Books, a division of Hodder Headline Limited, 338 Euston Road, London NW1 3BH

Picture acknowledgements: Rob Bowden 15, 35, 37, 57 (bottom); Howard Davies 48; Ecoscene 5 (L.A. Raman), 21 and 34
(Andrew Brown), 29 (Sally Morgan), 58 (Bruce Harber); Eye Ubiquitous 6 (Paul Thompson); HWPL 9, 11 (David Cumming),
55 (Richard Sharpley); Impact 26 (Mark Henley); Panos Pictures 4 and cover background (Peter Barker), 7 (Sean Sprague), 28
(Jean-Léo Dugast), 30 (Trevor Page), 45 (J.C. Tordai), 46 (Giacomo Pirozzi), 51 (Paul Harrison), 52 (Fred Hoogervorst), 53
(Jeremy Hartley), 57 (top) Jeremy Horner; Edward Parker 14; Popperfoto 10, 19 (Yun Suk-bong), 27 (George Mulala), 41, 47
(Daniel Aguilar); Still Pictures cover foreground (Hartmut Schwarzbach), 12 (DERA), 13 and 39 (Ron Giling), 16, 20 and 54
(Mark Edwards), 17 (Martin Pruneville), 18 (Albert Visage), 23 (Michael Gunther), 24 (Muriel Nicolotti), 38 (John Maier),
42 (Neil Cooper), 43 (E. Duigenan – Christian Aid), 59 (John Isaac); WTPix 32, 33 and 36 (Chris Fairclough).

Cover: foreground picture shows a mother and child in Fengdu, China; background picture shows a crowded street market in
Delhi, India.

CONTENTS

TOO MANY PEOPLE?

FACT

If you are about thirteen years old, a billion people have been added to the world's population since you were born.

By 2050 India will be the world's most populous country, contributing more than any other to our growing population.

Six billion and counting!

'At around midnight on Monday 11 October 1999 the world's six billionth person was born in Bosnia'
BBC News, 12 October 1999

We started the twenty-first century as a world of over six billion people, yet at the beginning of the twentieth century the world's population was only 1.65 billion. So, in just 100 years, the world's population had increased by an amazing 365 per cent, mostly between 1960 and 2000. Population growth is now slowing down, but there are still about 78 million more people every year. And it is predicted that there will be 9.5 billion of us by the end of the current century. Growth is expected to continue until some time around the year 2200 when the world population will probably stabilize at just over 10 billion people.

Pessimists and optimists

This rapid increase in population has been causing great concern for many years and the debate about whether or not the world is overpopulated continues. Some people argue that problems such as deforestation, climate change and famine show that the world does not have enough resources to support its current population. People who believe this are often known as 'pessimists' because of their negative views. They tell us that we must act to control population growth immediately if we are to avoid environmental disasters and human suffering.

Others, known as 'optimists', believe that people are the world's ultimate resource and will always find ways to cope. They argue that, as more people need to be fed, housed, educated and clothed, we will develop new ideas and inventions that make better use of resources or use newly discovered materials and technology. The optimists tell us that population growth will slow down naturally over time and that we need not panic.

This debate started over 200 years ago when the British economist Thomas Malthus warned that population was expanding faster than food supplies and would result in famine, disease and even war. However, improved agricultural techniques since then have allowed world food supplies to increase in line with population.

This crop, growing in India, is a specially developed High Yield Variety (HYV) of rice. HYVs have helped Asia avoid the mass famines predicted by Malthus.

VIEWPOINTS

'Population has come to evoke something threatening, something which casts a shadow over the future.'
Barbara Duden,
Institute for Cultural Studies, Essen, Germany

'We have two choices, and neither of them is to grow. We can let the limits themselves stop us, in their time and with complete indifference to our values. Or we can purposely slow down, ease back, become less wasteful and more efficient, contain the damage and preserve what is important to us'
Donella Meadows, co-author of The Limits to Growth and Beyond The Limits

Date	Population (billion)
1804	1
1927	2
1960	3
1974	4
1987	5
1999	6
2013*	7
2028*	8
2054*	9
2183*	10

* = estimates
Source: United Nations Population Division, 'The World at Six Billion'

A sustainable population

Attention is no longer focused on population purely in relation to food supply. The debate now centres on the relationship between population levels and the earth's limited resources. This approach to demography (the study of population) not only looks at the size of the population but also at the way people live and the resources their lifestyles use. The USA, for example, has a population of around 280 million, whereas India has 1,000 million (over three times as many people). But if we consider energy use then people living in the USA use over twenty-eight times more than those living in India. So, although the USA has fewer people, each of them has a bigger impact on the world's resources than a person living in India. This pattern is repeated across the world, with developed regions such as Europe, North America, Japan and Australia consuming around 80 per cent of global resources even though they account for just 20 per cent of the world's population.

The question is: what would happen if the majority of people living in developing areas were to live like those in developed regions? Environmentalists say the world could not support everyone living like an average American or European – it would be unsustainable. But we cannot expect people to accept that they have to continue living in poverty with poor healthcare and education facilities either. Many now argue that if resources were more fairly distributed there would be enough for everyone to enjoy a good standard of living. This means that we all need to think about our own

Mass consumption in developed nations, as in this shopping centre in Sydney, Australia, is placing enormous pressure on the earth's resources.

FACT

How much is a billion? If you were a billion seconds old you would be almost thirty-two. To travel a billion kilometres, you would have to travel around the world 24,975 times.

lives and how we can use fewer resources. If we all do this, there should be enough to go around both now and in the future. That is the basis of sustainable development.

The challenge ahead

This is not an easy task, however, as the number of people is growing all the time. In fact in the ten minutes it has taken you to read as far as this, the world's population will have grown by around another 1,500 people! By the end of this book you will have learned enough to form your own views on whether or not we really do live in an overcrowded world.

Changes in world population per hour (1955-2025)

Year	Births	Deaths	Natural increase
1955	11,500	5,800	5,700
1975	13,800	5,300	8,500
1995	15,100	5,900	9,200
2025*	15,500	7,500	8,000

*= estimate

Source: World Health Organization, World Health Report, 1998

VIEWPOINTS

'The unprecedented surge in population, combined with rising individual consumption, is pushing our claims on the planet beyond its natural limits.'
Lester Brown and others, Worldwatch Institute, USA

'Growing support for environmentally sustainable development is a positive sign that previously separate concerns for human development and environmental protection can be merged.'
Kate Chalkley, Population Reference Bureau, USA

A much lower-consumption lifestyle in Andhra Pradesh, India.

DEBATE

Before you read on, think about what you already know. What evidence shows that the world is overcrowded? What evidence suggests that population can keep growing without causing major problems? Which is most convincing?

A GROWING POPULATION

Calculating global population growth

FACT

In the UK, someone born in 1800 could expect to live to the age of thirty-six, someone born in 1900 would probably live to fifty. The average person born in 2000 will live seventy-seven years.

Population grows when the number of people being born is greater than the number of people dying in a particular period. For example, if 1,000 new babies were born in a year, and 950 people died in the same year, then the population would have grown by 50. If the original population was 2,000 then the growth rate would be 2.5 per cent per year. In reality, the fastest the world population has ever grown was 2.04 per cent in the late 1960s. Today it is growing at around 1.31 per cent per year.

Does population growth vary?

There is a great deal of variation between regions of the world, and also between countries within a particular region. Africa currently has the highest regional population growth rate at 2.4 per cent per year, with countries like The Gambia (3.6 per cent) and Kenya (3.4 per cent) growing particularly fast. The highest rates in the world are those of some Middle Eastern countries such as Saudi Arabia and Oman whose populations are currently growing at around 4.5 per cent each year. Europe has the lowest population growth rate (less than 0.5 per cent), and in some countries, such as Italy, Greece, Portugal, Bulgaria and Hungary, populations are now reducing.

One problem with calculating national population growth is that people sometimes move from country to country for work or other reasons. So, in addition to births and deaths, we need to consider the number of people moving in and out of a country.

Healthier and older

The rapid increase in population during the twentieth century (particularly in the second half) was mainly due to people being healthier and living longer. A person born today can expect to live for sixty-six years, on average, whereas those born in 1950 were only expected to live forty-six years. Today, around 10 per cent of the world's population is over sixty, and this is expected to increase to 22 per cent by 2050. Europe will be the oldest region, with one in three people (35 per cent) over sixty, compared to Africa, the youngest region, where it will be just one in every eight (12 per cent).

VIEWPOINT

'[It is] useless, these days, for children to learn populations of countries. By the time they're asked again, the answer will be different'
Paul Harrison, The Third Revolution, *1992*

Improvements in healthcare mean that people are living much longer, especially in European countries. This couple are from Greece.

VIEWPOINTS

'Had birth rates not fallen in the latter half of the 20th century, world population would be 2.3 billion higher than it is today.'
Population Action International, 'People in the Balance', 2000

'At some time in the 1970s, humanity as a whole passed the point at which it lived within the global regenerative capacity of the Earth.'
World Wide Fund For Nature, 'Living Planet Report 2000'

These dramatic improvements in life expectancy are due to many factors, but three developments have been particularly important:

Improvements in modern medicine

Since the 1950s medical science has developed vaccines to protect us against diseases such as polio, measles, tuberculosis, tetanus and smallpox. These illnesses had previously killed many people, particularly young children under five. Medicine has also enabled us to keep people alive for longer, using modern surgery and powerful drugs. The development of antibiotics, such as penicillin, to help fight infections has been one of the most significant improvements.

Increasing access to sanitation and clean water

The introduction of sewers and protected water sources has had a significant impact on people's health since 1950. In developed regions, these improvements in hygiene have almost eliminated the spread of diseases (such as cholera, typhus and diarrhoea) caused by contaminated water. But in developing countries lack of sanitation still causes

Health standards remain poor in many developing countries: these open sewers are in Jakarta, capital of Indonesia.

many deaths. In parts of Africa, for example, over half the population has no access to clean water, hygienic lavatories and washing facilities.

Rising incomes and living standards

Better education and higher incomes have dramatically improved living standards in the developed world. People are better informed about nutrition and hygiene and have access to affordable medical facilities. In contrast, many developing countries still have a very high mortality (death) rate. This is partly due to disease but also largely due to lack of education, income and medical facilities. In Mozambique, for example, 206 out of every 1,000 children will die before they reach the age of five, compared to less than 8 per 1,000 in countries such as the USA, the UK, Denmark and Japan.

Education, especially of girls, has been proven to reduce population growth dramatically.

Population momentum

Even though population growth rates have decreased, the number of people is still growing rapidly. This is because the many young people who were born when growth was at its highest are now having children of their own. In East Africa, for instance, around half the population is under eighteen years of age. As they begin to have children of their own, the region's population is expected to more than double from 97 million in 1999 to 228 million by 2050. This increase in numbers is known as 'population momentum' and will only slow down when parents choose to have fewer children.

FACT

Between 2000 and 2050, Italy's population is expected to fall from 57 million to 41 million, while Japan's is predicted to decrease from 127 million to 105 million.

DEBATE

How many children were there in your grandparents' family or even further back? How many are there in your parents' family and in your own? Now think about your ideal family size in the future. What trends can you identify in population growth? Why do you think this is?

POPULATION AND RESOURCES

Not enough to go around?

VIEWPOINT

'The resource that worries me most is the declining capacity of the planet to buffer itself against human impacts.'
Paul Ehrlich, 1990

Those most concerned about population growth tell us that there are simply not enough resources on earth to go around. This would be particularly worrying if everyone was to consume resources like those currently living in developed regions. Friends of the Earth suggest that if, in 2050, everyone lived the same lifestyle as people in the UK today, we would need 1.5 planets to provide enough land, 3.5 planets for wood, 4.5 for cement, 5.5 for steel, and over 8 planets to provide enough aluminium and energy.

Images of earth, from space, have alerted people to the fragile nature of our planet and its limited resources.

Others believe that new discoveries, improved technology and more efficient use of existing resources will ensure that there is enough for everyone in the future. More efficient motor vehicles and the use of renewable energy sources, such as solar or wind power, are examples of these changes. Another example is aluminium drinks cans. These use 85 per cent less material in their manufacture now than they did in 1935. In Europe, however, around 60 per cent of aluminium cans were thrown away in 1998. These could have been recycled to save on both the resources and energy used in manufacturing with raw materials.

Betting the world

In 1980 two scientists made a very famous bet about population and resources. Paul Ehrlich (a pessimist) believed that population growth would lead to shortages in resources and cause their price to increase as they became scarce. Julian Simon (an optimist) believed that technological advances would mean there would be no shortage of resources and that prices would in fact decrease. Paul Ehrlich chose five metals (chrome, copper, nickel, tin and tungsten) to test their different views over a ten-year period. By 1990 the metals had all declined in price. So Julian Simon won the bet, even though world population had increased by 800 million. He claimed this proved that people will always manage to overcome resource problems and that population growth is not a problem. Paul Ehrlich admitted losing the bet, but still believes that population growth will cause resource shortages in the future.

Copper, being mined here in Zambia, was one of the metals in the Paul Ehrlich and Julian Simon bet. The price of copper fell over a ten-year period, proving – according to Simon – that population growth should not be a major concern.

FACT

Paper consumption increased by 86 per cent between 1961 and 1994, requiring the clearance of 16 million hectares of forest every year.

A reforestation programme in Tanzania – just one way of overcoming resource scarcity.

Overcoming resource scarcity

Humans can overcome scarcity of some resources more easily than others. For instance, certain resources are renewable, such as forests which can be replanted after the trees have been removed. In reality, however, forests are often cleared with little thought of replanting. So even renewable resources can become scarce. Other resources such as oil, coal and minerals, like copper, bauxite (used to make aluminium) and iron ore (used to make steel), are non-renewable. When they are taken from the ground we are unable to replace them, as it takes millions of years for them to be formed.

Renewable resources

The earth has many renewable resources including forests, water, soil and wildlife. These replace themselves naturally over time and have done so

FACT

The amount of water available per person from the hydrological cycle (evaporation and rainfall) is expected to fall by 73 per cent between 1950 and 2050 due to population growth.

for millions of years, but humans have altered this natural balance. The growth in total population and the increased demands of individuals have placed enormous pressure on the world's renewable resources. Global forests, for example, halved from 1.2 hectares per person in 1960 to 0.6 hectares by 1996, and they are expected to fall to 0.4 hectares per person by 2025.

Although much of this decline is due to population growth, it is also caused by poor management of forest resources. For instance, between 1980 and 1995 around 180 million hectares of forest were cleared but only 20 million hectares were planted. Most of the clearance took place in developing countries where populations are growing most rapidly, while nearly all the planting was in developed nations. Developing countries may not have the money to plant trees when they are struggling to provide housing and schooling for their growing populations. It is also important to realize that much of the forest clearance in developing areas provides materials for people living in developed countries and is not for local use at all.

Even when efforts are made to renew resources it takes time. Fast-growing trees need around twenty-five years before they can be harvested, yet in this length of time the world population could increase by 2 billion people!

VIEWPOINTS

'Despite innovative approaches to dealing with changes in natural-resource supply, the reality is that supplies of these resources are finite.'
Population Action International, 'People in the Balance'

'The world's oil companies are now finding only one barrel of oil for every four that we consume.'
Colin Campbell, oil geologist, quoted in New Scientist

A tree nursery at Sebit, in northern Kenya, provides mango seedlings to help farmers conserve their environment.

Non-renewable resources

Many of the resources on which we rely most are non-renewable. The petrol for our vehicles, the coal and gas that produces our electricity, and the many minerals that provide us with building materials and modern consumer goods are all non-renewable. For instance, the known oil reserves of Denmark are predicted to run out by around 2010, while those of the USA and UK are expected to run out even earlier. So what will happen then? Wealthy countries will probably import oil from countries with bigger reserves such as those of the Middle East, but poorer nations may only be able to do this by further increasing their debts.

Oil, being extracted here in Cuba, is a major non-renewable resource on which we rely. Once used, it cannot be replaced.

Environmentalists believe that we should stop using fossil fuels such as oil now and not wait for it to run out before we look for alternatives. They tell us that more people using more fuel will lead to global warming and pollution, and that even if we were to stop tomorrow we would still suffer some warming of the climate. There are also environmental risks in transporting oil over large distances. In 1989 the oil tanker *Exxon Valdez* spilled 240,000 barrels of oil in waters off Alaska, damaging the local ecology and people's livelihoods. And in Nigeria oil pipelines have leaked and even exploded several times in recent years, destroying farmland and killing people.

FACT

In 1997, 25 per cent of the world's 501 million private cars were registered in the USA.

How important is population?

Population growth clearly places additional pressure on the world's resources, but is it really the most important cause of such shortages? Many people now think not and instead blame the consumer lifestyles of people living in developed regions. For example, an American child will have generated 52 tonnes of rubbish, used 886 million litres of water and used five times more energy than the world average by the time they reach their life expectancy of seventy-five years.

Greater use of renewable energy, higher rates of recycling and less wasteful consumption are all ways in which the developed world could reduce its impact on global resources. The development of modern information technology, such as computers and the internet, was expected to help by reducing the amount of paper that was consumed. However, a recent study in the USA suggested that the use of paper in offices had increased by 40 per cent following the introduction of e-mail as people print out their messages.

VIEWPOINT

'Even total success in eliminating deforestation would fail to ensure an increase in forest resources unless equal success is achieved in slowing population growth.'
Population Action International. 'Forest Futures', 1999

The transportation of oil has caused several environmental disasters. Here teams are cleaning a beach after the Erika oil disaster in France, December 1999.

DEBATE

Looking at your own use of resources during a normal day, how many of them are renewable and how many are non-renewable? How sustainable do you think your own resource use is?

POPULATION AND THE ENVIRONMENT

Links between population and environment

Growing populations in developing regions and over-consuming populations in developed regions are often blamed by environmentalists for problems such as global warming, deforestation and threats to wildlife. However, the environment can also place pressure on the human population and may even be responsible for population growth in some places. For example, in tropical environments where mosquitoes are common, many young children die of malaria (a parasitic disease spread by the bites of mosquitoes). Because of this, parents often have many children in order to make sure that some will survive. Other areas, such as the Nile Valley, attract people because they have good fertile soil and are therefore densely populated.

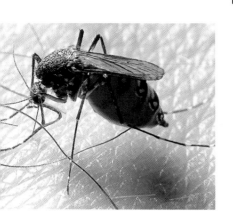

In areas where mosquitoes carry life-threatening malaria, population growth is often higher to ensure a better chance of survival.

The links between population and the environment are very complicated, but scientists agree that we must try to understand them. Most importantly, we need to understand when population growth threatens the environment and when the environment affects population growth.

Carrying capacity

Scientists often study the links between population and environment by measuring what's known as the 'carrying capacity' of a region. The carrying capacity means the amount of life that any particular ecosystem (a pond, forest, country or the planet) can support sustainably. Some scientists have suggested that the earth's carrying capacity is as low as 3 billion people and others have placed it as high as 44 billion. So who is right? If 3 billion is the right number then we are already at twice our sustainable limit. But if 44 billion is correct then our population can afford to increase a further seven times, which at current rates would take almost 155 years. The real figure is probably somewhere in between, and as population growth is expected to stabilize at about 10 billion there is hope that we will be able to build a sustainable future.

New technologies and our behaviour (which constantly changes our relationship with the natural environment) make it hard to calculate carrying capacity. Cleaner fuels and the use of catalytic converters, for example, mean that new cars produce less than half the emissions they did twenty years ago. However, if a family now has two cars, their overall environmental impact is probably greater because of the materials and energy used in manufacturing the second car.

VIEWPOINTS

'Population pressures and a lack of adequate agricultural technologies, among other factors, are major forces driving the poor to make desperate choices.'
Professor Gordon Conway, environmentalist and former vice-chancellor of the University of Sussex, UK

'Saying that the Netherlands is thriving with a [population] density of 1,180 people per square mile simply ignores that those 1,180 Dutch people far exceed the carrying capacity of that square mile.'
Paul and Anne Ehrlich, The Population Explosion, 1990

Modern cars are less damaging to the environment but we are now producing and driving more cars than ever before. This car factory is in South Korea, a country where car ownership is growing rapidly.

Water and carrying capacity

It is easier to consider carrying capacity when looking at a particular resource. Water is essential for human life and, although it is a renewable resource, it is also finite (globally limited) and can

take a long time to be renewed by nature. In many parts of the world, growing human demand is causing serious water shortages. Globally, the demand for fresh water increased by 400 per cent between 1940 and 1990, almost twice as fast as population growth. In the year 2000 some 505 million people were living with water shortages. By 2025 this could increase to 3.2 billion – around 40 per cent of world population.

Drilling for water in Jordan, one of several countries that is using water faster than it can be replaced.

Carrying capacities for water are most seriously exceeded in several Middle Eastern states which have some of the lowest natural supplies of water (due to their hot, dry climate) while having the highest population growth rates in the world. Saudi Arabia, for example, has just 111 cubic metres of water per person, which falls far short of the recommended global minimum of 1,700 cubic metres. With its current population growth rate of 4.6 per cent, it is expected that the amount of water available in Saudi Arabia will fall to just 60 cubic metres per person by 2025. The Democratic Republic of the Congo (DRC), by contrast, is expected to have around 150,000 cubic metres per person in 2025 even though its population is also growing rapidly, at 3.3 per cent per year. This is because much of the DRC is covered in rainforest that receives some of the highest annual rainfall in the world.

VIEWPOINT

'Our planet has more than enough fresh water for every living person; it is often just in the wrong place at the wrong time.'
Joel Cohen, Rockefeller University Laboratory of Populations, New York, USA

Extending carrying capacity

When the carrying capacity of a particular resource is exceeded, many countries simply import more of it from countries that still have plenty. But this can be very costly so it only tends to be an option for wealthier nations. Many environmentalists would also argue that it fools people into thinking their lifestyles are sustainable, when in fact they are simply using up someone else's resources. An alternative is to replace the scarce resource with one that is more plentiful. Countries such as Denmark and Germany have begun to do this, by switching from fossil fuels to using renewable wind and solar power to satisfy their energy needs.

VIEWPOINTS

'Demand for fresh water in many places now exceeds supply. Conflicts resulting from water shortages could become very serious in parts of the Middle East, China and India in the years to come.'
Population Reference Bureau, 'World Population: more than just numbers', 1999

'Because the growth of world population is slowing significantly the future looks less water-short than it did in 1993.'
Population Action International, 'People in the Balance', 2000

FACT

A child born in the USA consumes 30–40 times more natural resources than a child born in a developing country such as India.

Irrigation in the Owens Valley, California, USA. Irrigation has improved food supplies dramatically but places great pressure on water resources.

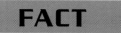

FACT

Over-fishing of Nile perch from Lake Victoria means that fish now frequently weigh as little as 0.8 kg, compared to a fully grown fish, which can weigh as much as 200 kg.

VIEWPOINTS

'In 50 years, if we don't change the management of reserves in developing countries where most biodiversity resides, it will be too late. Ultimately nature and biodiversity must be conserved for their own sakes.'
Andrew Balmford, University of Cambridge

'It is simply no good to tell the head of a starving family...not to cut down trees for firewood, or not to burn the forest to clear land for more... cultivation. Such postures are worthless, arrogant, simplistic and doomed to failure.'
Niles Eldredge, American Museum of Natural History, New York

Carrying capacity can also be extended by using resources more efficiently. Improved production techniques and higher levels of recycling are just two ways in which this can be achieved. We can also use resources more efficiently in our own daily lives. Taking a shower instead of a bath, for example, reduces water use by about 60 per cent and every tonne of paper we recycle saves about fifteen trees.

Population and wildlife

Our use of habitats around the world for housing, industry, agriculture and energy production means that we are now placing greater pressure on wildlife than at any time in human history. For instance, in recent years over-fishing in Lake Victoria, East Africa, has led to smaller and smaller fish being caught. Their small size means many of them have not bred yet. So future fish stocks are likely to decline even further, threatening not just the fish but also the people who rely on fishing for their survival. The same is happening in the North Atlantic fisheries of Europe, leading to limits being placed on how much fish (especially cod) can be caught.

Globally, it is estimated that fifty plant species become extinct every day and around two-thirds of the world's bird species are endangered, with 10 per cent at serious risk of extinction. Some groups of animals, such as the primates (gorillas, chimpanzees and monkeys), are under particular threat. If their habitats continue to be destroyed at current rates, at least 120 of the 620 primate species will probably become extinct before 2025.

Unfortunately, the places on earth with the greatest biodiversity (number and variety of species) are mainly located in developing regions where population growth is highest. Their governments have the difficult job of deciding how best to protect the environment while also allowing their people to use it to improve their standard of living. In many countries this is done by creating protected areas such as national parks or game reserves. Denmark and Norway, for example, have both set aside over 30 per cent of their land as protected areas. However, Denmark and Norway have less than 3,000 species, of which fewer than 30 are threatened. Brazil, by contrast, has over 58,000 species, of which over 1,500 are threatened. Yet only 4.2 per cent of Brazil's land area is protected.

VIEWPOINTS

Any long-term solution to the growing imbalance between fish resources and human demands will require not only innovative approaches to conservation and management but also an early end to population growth.'
Population Action International, 'People in the Balance', 2000

'In 1995, 301,000 Japanese fishers produced 6.7 million tons of fish while it took nearly six million small-scale Indian fishers to produce about five million tons.'
New Internationalist *magazine*

Primate species, such as mountain gorillas in Rwanda, are endangered by the growth and activities of local human populations.

FACT

Masai protests in Kenya's Amboseli National Park during the 1980s led to the killing of 95 per cent of its already endangered rhino population.

The Masai of East Africa have co-existed with wildlife for centuries. This balance now is threatened by population growth and changing land use.

People and wildlife in conflict

In some regions people have come into direct conflict with wildlife. In Kenya, the Masai people and local wildlife have traditionally shared their environment. But since the 1970s areas of Masai land have been set aside as national parks to protect wildlife and encourage tourism. The Masai's herding activities became restricted and they felt angry that they did not share in the money made from tourism. When the government ignored their concerns in the late 1980s the Masai started killing wildlife as a protest. Fortunately the Kenya Wildlife Service is now working with the Masai to set up projects that protect wildlife while also providing the Masai with an income from sustainable tourism. Kimana Community Wildlife Sanctuary is the best known of these and its success is now leading to the establishment of similar projects.

Global warming – the ultimate test

Experts now agree that the ultimate test of the link between people and environment is the threat of global warming. Our expanding population is producing more and more of the greenhouse gases that cause global warming. Carbon dioxide (CO_2), one of the most important greenhouse gases, is produced when fossil fuels are burned to provide energy for our homes, factories and transport; global CO_2 emissions increased almost twice as fast as population between 1950 and 1998. Scientists believe that this could contribute to some countries warming by as much as 6°C over the next 100 years.

These warmer temperatures are expected to change weather patterns, causing floods, droughts and severe storms across the planet. Sea levels are also expected to rise by up to 1 metre, threatening coastal areas and low-lying islands. Developed nations are responsible for 75 per cent of the increase in CO_2 emissions since 1950. However, between 1990 and 1998 their emissions increased by just 8 per cent, compared to a 39 per cent increase from developing nations. This suggests that developing countries with their rapidly growing populations, combined with rising living standards and rapid industrialization, may soon become the biggest contributors to global warming. It is therefore essential to use cleaner energies to power the development of these countries without destroying the environment – but who will pay for them?

VIEWPOINTS

'Due to the rapidly increasing size of the populations and economies of countries like China, India and Mexico, greenhouse gas emissions from developing countries will soon pose a significant threat to global climate.'
Joy Fishel, Zero Population Growth, USA

'The most important causes of ozone depletion are consumption patterns and industry, not population growth.'
Kate Chalkley, Population Reference Bureau, USA

DEBATE

Although one individual's impact on our environment may be small, the combined effect of lots of people can be significant. Take some time to consider your own personal impacts, in terms of what you eat, buy and do with your leisure time. Should you try to reduce the impact of any of these activities? Why?

FEEDING THE WORLD'S POPULATION

FACT

The world has an estimated 1.5 billion hectares of land suitable for farming, but less than half of this is used to produce food.

Obesity is a growing problem in more developed countries, while in developing regions, millions go hungry every day.

A hungry world?

As we begin the twenty-first century, an estimated 1 billion people (1 in 6 of the world's population) do not get enough food to eat each day. Most of them live in developing regions: South Asia and sub-Saharan Africa are the areas where hunger is greatest. India alone has an estimated 200 million hungry people (around 20 per cent of its population) and in some of the poorest countries in the world, such as Mozambique, Haiti and Somalia, over half the population goes hungry each day. Some experts argue that this proves the world is overpopulated and failing to feed itself, but others say this argument is too simple. They point out that there is more than enough food in most developed nations, and that the real problem is that people are eating too much. In the USA, for example, 55 per cent of adults are overweight – twice as many as in 1960 – and in Canada and the UK the number of obese people has doubled in the last ten years alone. So is the world really hungry?

Food aid has been needed periodically to avoid mass starvation in countries such as Ethiopia, pictured here. But is this a result of population growth?

World food supplies

In 1798 Thomas Malthus warned that food supplies could not keep pace with population growth. He said that population grew geometrically (2, 4, 8, 16, 32 ... etc), but food supply could only grow arithmetically (1, 2, 3, 4, 5 ... etc), meaning that population would soon outstrip food supply. In reality new farming techniques, including the use of machinery, irrigation and fertilizers, have enabled us to grow more food – even with rapidly expanding populations. In fact, since the 1970s, global food supply per person has increased by 20 per cent, despite the addition of a further 2.3 billion people (more than 8 USAs or 40 UKs or 430 Denmarks!). Growth in food production is expected to fall over the next thirty years, from 2.2 per cent per year at present to 1.5 per cent by 2030. However, this figure is still higher than the population growth rate, which is currently 1.3 per cent and expected to decrease further in the future.

VIEWPOINTS

'Easing world hunger could become unimaginably difficult if population growth resembles demographers' higher projections.'
Population Action International. 'Why Population Matters to Natural Resources'

'...there is no reason not to have a hunger-free world some time in the next century. The world already produces enough food to feed the people who inhabit it today. And it could produce more.'
Jacques Diouf. Food and Agricultural Organization, Italy

FACT

In the mid-1990s developing nations imported around 107 million tonnes of cereals (such as wheat and maize) from developed nations; this is expected to increase to 270 million tonnes per year by 2030.

Inequalities in food supply

If there is enough food in the world, why are 6 million children dying each year because of malnutrition? And why do millions more suffer from diseases and disabilities associated with food shortages? One reason is that world food supplies are very unevenly distributed. The average food availability in developing regions is currently around 2,100 calories per person per day, but as low as 1,532 in Somalia (the world's lowest). In developed nations, by contrast, the average is 3,200 calories per day. Denmark has the highest in the world at 3,808 calories per person per day, almost two and a half times more than an average Somalian.

But the differences are not just global. In Brazil over 30 per cent of people are overweight, while millions of others are malnourished and struggle to find one meal a day. And in the USA, which has the highest proportion of overweight people, around 5 million households are reported to suffer from hunger, 800,000 of them with severe food shortages. So why do these inequalities exist?

Luxury foods, such as this French-style bread being sold in Tra Vinh market, Vietnam, often rely on expensive imported grains. This can harm the market for local produce such as rice.

Wealthier nations overcome food shortages by purchasing food from countries with a surplus. Here, wheat is being loaded for transportation from a silo in Virginia, USA.

The cost of food

The price of food is perhaps the most important factor. Wealthy individuals and nations can afford to buy food if they face shortages, but for millions of people living in poverty there is no such option. These wealthy nations are sometimes criticized for buying food from elsewhere because much of the best land in developing countries is used to grow food for export instead of feeding their own growing populations. On the other hand, the money earned from exporting food helps development and provides people with jobs and an income. But studies have shown that buying food, instead of growing it, can be very expensive for developing countries. In Bangladesh, Tanzania and Vietnam around 60 per cent of household income is spent on food, making it by far the biggest expense. By comparison, around 20 per cent is spent on food in wealthier nations such as Australia, France and Japan, with more being spent on recreation and consumer goods such as computers, music and cosmetics.

VIEWPOINT

'...future food production increases will have to come from higher yields. And though I have no doubt yields will keep going up, whether they can go up enough to feed the population monster is another matter.'
Norman Borlaug, Green Revolution scientist and Nobel Peace Prize winner

Food aid donated by France being unloaded at Mogadishu port in Somalia.

Food aid

For the past fifty years much effort has been directed into trying to meet the food demands of the world's population. Surplus food from one area is sometimes sent to other areas that lack supplies. This 'food aid' is often provided after disasters such as the devastating floods in Mozambique in February 2000 which destroyed crops and food stores. Without food aid, millions of people could have faced starvation. However, food aid is rarely beneficial in the long term; it is better for countries to grow their own food where possible.

FACT

350,000 children go blind each year due to lack of vitamin A in their diets. GM rice, known as 'golden rice', which contains vitamin A, could help reduce this.

Increasing food supplies

Countries can increase their food supplies by importing food, but for many of the poorest countries this can result in large debts that threaten the development of services such as health and education. In the 1960s scientists developed new crops called High Yield Varieties (HYV) to try to improve food supplies in developing countries. HYV crops produced more seed than traditional varieties, allowing farmers to grow more food on the same land. When famine-struck India and Pakistan introduced HYV wheat and rice in the mid-1960s, yields increased by over 75 per cent, making both countries self-sufficient in food by 1974. This dramatic improvement became known as 'The Green Revolution'.

HYV seeds are expensive though, and require large amounts of fertilizers and pesticides that poor farmers cannot always afford. They also require regular water supplies, which often means introducing water artificially (irrigation). Only 17 per cent of the world's cropland is irrigated, but it produces 40 per cent of all crops and its importance is growing every year. However, irrigation often wastes a lot of water; up to 90 per cent of the water may fail to reach the crops due to leaks and evaporation in hot climates.

Genetic engineering and food supply

The most recent development to increase food supplies is the use of genetic engineering to produce Genetically Modified Organisms (GMOs); scientists alter the genes of plants and animals to make them grow stronger and resist diseases. Although this could provide the answer to future food supply problems, many people are against it because they think it is 'tampering with nature'. They argue that scientists do not know enough about the long-term effects of such technology both on the environment and human health. For many hungry people, however, that may be a risk worth taking!

VIEWPOINTS

'Strong opposition to genetically modified food (GM food) in the European Union has resulted in severe restrictions for modern biotechnology for agriculture.'
International Food Policy Research Institute

'It would be unethical to condemn future generations to hunger by refusing to develop and apply a technology that can build on what our forefathers provided and can help produce adequate food for a world with almost 2 billion more people by 2020.'
Richard Flavell, Ceres Inc. USA

DEBATE

Next time you visit the supermarket, look at the labels to see where the food you eat comes from. What are the good and bad points about eating food grown in other countries?

POPULATION AND LIVING SPACE

Running out of room?

During the 1960s some demographers tried to imagine what the world would be like if population continued to double at the then predicted rate of once every thirty-seven years. They suggested that in 900 years there would be 60 quadrillion people (60,000,000,000,000,000) – about 100 people for every square metre (about the size of a phone booth). In such a world people would live vertically in 2,000-storey buildings that covered the whole planet.

A crowded street in Shanghai, one of China's most densely populated cities.

Thankfully, such predictions did not come true. The doubling from 2 to 4 billion actually took forty-seven years (1927 to 1974) and the next doubling to 8 billion is expected in 2028, fifty-four years later. But there are still concerns about our living space, and these should not be ignored. When you are stuck in traffic or trying to squeeze through a bustling crowd you may think the world is already running out of living space, but how crowded is it really?

Hong Kong in China has one of the highest population densities in the world.

VIEWPOINT

'Because the US is the fastest growing industrialized country and our consumption habits are disproportionately higher than citizens of most other countries, the nation stands as the most overpopulated country in the world.'
Zero Population Growth, 'Living in a Material World'

Population density

We measure how crowded a place is by calculating its 'population density'. This is the number of people living in a particular area and is normally measured as people per square kilometre (km^2). Globally, there were about 44 people per km^2 in 1999, and this is expected to increase to around 66 per km^2 by 2050. This global average hides great differences though. The USA, for example, is below the average with 29 people per km^2, whereas Denmark and the UK are above the average with 123 and 241 respectively. The most crowded regions in 1999 were Singapore (5,699 per km^2), Hong Kong (6,508 per km^2) and the Chinese province of Macau with an amazing 25,942 people per km^2. The least crowded countries included Canada, Botswana, Australia and Mongolia with less than 4 people per km^2.

Population density also varies within a country. Mountains, forests and deserts often have few inhabitants, whereas cities and coastal areas are usually more crowded. China, for instance, has an average population density of 132 people per km^2, but Shanghai, one of its biggest cities, has about 2,350 people per km^2.

FACT

The population of Dhaka, the capital of Bangladesh, grew at an average annual rate of 6.9 per cent per year between 1975 and 2000 – more than double the national average.

VIEWPOINT

'...increased population density can induce the necessary social and technical changes to bring about better living standards...'
Mary Tiffen, population researcher and author

A space crisis

Finding room for everyone to live is a major challenge. If an average home houses six people, for example, then we need to build 13 million new homes every year to keep up with population growth – more than all the houses in Australia, Ireland, New Zealand and South Africa combined. In rural areas in many developing countries young people (normally boys) are given part of their parents' land when they start their own families. As populations have grown, however, each family has been left with a smaller and smaller piece of land, making it harder for them to grow enough food for a healthy diet. In Kenya the amount of cropland per person more than halved between 1975 and 2000. This pressure on land has forced many to move away from rural areas to towns and cities in a process known as 'urbanization'.

An urbanizing world

The twenty-first century will be remembered as the urban century because there will be more of us living in urban areas than rural areas for the first time in history. Europe, North America, Latin America, Oceania, and South-East Asia have been

Luxury homes like these, in suburban Bel Air, California, are an example of extravagant use of living space.

FACT

In 1999 Tokyo was the biggest mega-city with nearly 29 million people – almost 5 million more than the entire population of Scandinavia (Denmark, Finland, Iceland, Norway and Sweden).

Urban population growth is particularly rapid in many developing countries. Here in Cairo, Egypt, the authorities have difficulty in controlling the quality and expansion of living space.

more urban than rural since 1975, while South Asia and sub-Saharan Africa are expected to remain mostly rural until around 2030. Individual cities have grown particularly fast in the last fifty years. Some, with populations of over 10 million people, have become known as mega-cities. These are mainly located in developing countries, with Tokyo (Japan), New York and Los Angeles (USA) being notable exceptions. Mexico City (Mexico), Sao Paulo (Brazil), Mumbai and Calcutta (India), Lagos (Nigeria) and Shanghai (China) are among the biggest at present and many of them are still growing rapidly. Lagos in Nigeria, for example, is expected to double in size between 1999 and 2015 to accommodate at least 25 million people.

But what does urbanization mean for population growth and our impact on the planet? Many scientists believe that cities are the most efficient way for people to live, but others believe they encourage an over-consuming lifestyle that threatens our environment.

FACT

In developing countries the number of mega-cities (cities with populations of more than 10 million) is expected to increase from ten in 2000 to twenty-two by 2020.

FACT

New York's Fresh-Kills urban-waste landfill is so large it can be seen from outer space! It has now been closed.

Efficient cities?

Higher population density in cities means that services such as public transport and water can be more easily provided than in areas where people live far apart. In the UK, for example, buses on city routes may depart every 10 minutes, but rural villages often have only one or two buses a week. This means that many rural people travel in their own vehicles, using more resources and creating more pollution than city-dwellers.

Services such as public transport are often more efficient in urban areas (such as here in Hong Kong), due to the higher population density and demand.

Cities often have better health and education facilities too, and offer greater job opportunities and higher wages than rural areas. These can help control population growth because women who are well educated, healthy and wealthier are known to have fewer children. In Brazil, for instance, women who have completed secondary school have an average of 2.5 children, compared to 6.5 for women with little or no schooling. Urban areas also provide better financial services such as banking

Providing services to remote regions, such as Turkana district in Kenya, is difficult and expensive due to low population densities.

and insurance. These can improve people's lives and reduce the need for larger families which traditionally provided such support.

But cities can also be crowded and congested: traffic moves slowly and fills the air with choking exhaust fumes that sting your eyes, give you headaches and make breathing difficult. Services may collapse under the pressure of so many people, and crime can become a problem as the very rich and very poor struggle to live side by side. Some believe city life encourages people to buy more, in order to keep up with the newest fashions and trends. This consumer lifestyle demands enormous resources and produces mountains of waste. Some environmentalists even refer to cities as parasites that suck the life from the countryside. This is because they consume resources from distant rural areas and even from different countries – rather like a ripple that spreads outwards when you drop a stone into water. Looking down from above on Khartoum, in the Sudan, for example, this 'ripple' can be seen as a ring of deforestation stretching for over 100 km around the city. All the trees in this area have been cleared to provide wood and charcoal for fuel.

VIEWPOINT

'Urban inhabitants in some cases consume a disproportionate percentage of total fuelwood. Thus an inhabitant of Dakar [Senegal] draws, on average, 2–3 times as much from national wood resources as a rural inhabitant.'
W. Floor and J. Gorse, World Bank report, 'Household energy issues in West Africa'

VIEWPOINTS

'Staying alive in the shanty town demands a certain "selfishness" that pits individuals against each other and that rewards those who take advantage of those even weaker.'
Nancy Scheper-Hughes,
Death Without Weeping.
1992

'...there is an enormous potential among the large desperately poor populations of mega-cities. We must find ways of harnessing this energy to make cities more productive and to ensure a better life for these workers and their children.'
Saskia Sassen and S. Patel,
quoted in Urban Age. 1996

Curitiba's public transport system: a key part of the sustainable city.

Can developing cities cope?

Many cities in developing countries appear to be overwhelmed by their growing populations. With governments unable to keep pace, people have built their own communities on the edges of the cities or on empty land within the city boundaries. These are called squatter settlements, but are also sometimes known as shanty towns, favelas (in Brazil), bidonvilles or slums. They are usually built without permission and lack facilities such as clean water, sewage disposal, waste collection and electricity. As a result, people living in these communities often suffer from illnesses such as diarrhoea, cholera and typhoid. Children are especially vulnerable because they frequently play near piles of waste and open sewers. Many may be worse off than those living in rural areas, especially if their parents are unable to find work.

Sustainable cities

Experts agree that more of us will live in cities in the future and that they will have to become more sustainable. A good example of a sustainable city is Curitiba in Brazil which has a population of around 2 million. Curitiba's city authorities have managed population growth by providing an efficient public

transport network and controlling where people build: high-density housing is built near good transport services to ensure that people can move around efficiently. Curitiba also has an advanced waste recycling scheme where residents separate out over 150 tonnes of recyclable waste every day for collection by the 'garbage that is not garbage' lorry. Even the poorest residents in the favelas are included, swapping bags of collected rubbish for bus tickets or food vouchers. This scheme has reduced disease considerably and has improved both the environment and the quality of people's lives.

Many believe that more cities will have to become like Curitiba if they are to provide safe, healthy homes for their growing populations without harming the environment. Globally, living space does not appear to be a problem. But when large numbers of people come together in one urban centre they place great pressure on the immediate area. This is why cities will need to change in the future.

Urban slums in Buenos Aires, Argentina.

FACT

By 2050 it is estimated that 6.2 billion people – more than the entire global population in the year 2000 – will live in cities.

DEBATE

Would you rather live in a rural or urban area? Why would you rather live there? And how would your decision affect your impact on the environment?

POVERTY AND POPULATION

Does having too many children cause poverty?

Many believe that people in developing countries are poor because they have too many children – too many mouths to feed. There is some evidence that this is true. For example, in Denmark where the fertility rate (average number of children born per woman) is 1.7, the average annual income is almost US$35,000 per person. By comparison, Israel with a fertility rate of 2.7 has an average income of around US$16,000 per person and Uganda, with one of the highest fertility rates in the world at 7.1 children per woman, has an average income of just US$330.

But there are several countries that challenge this pattern. For example, Cuba has a fertility rate of only 1.6, compared to the USA where women have an average of 2 children each. But the average annual income in Cuba is just US$1,540, compared to almost US$30,000 in the USA. If there was really a direct connection then Cuba would be wealthier than the USA. So what is the real link between poverty and population?

Why do poor people have many children?

Many experts believe that people have many children because they are poor and that population growth will only slow down if we first focus on reducing poverty. So why is this? Those living in poverty usually suffer poor diets and living conditions, leading to a higher rate of illness and death. In Uganda, for example, nearly 14 per cent

VIEWPOINTS

'Families will not reduce their numbers of births until they are sure that the births they do have will result in surviving children.'
Margaret Catley-Carlson, President of Population Council

'Rather than being poor because they have many children, people may have many children because they are poor.'
Tom Hewitt and Ines Smyth, quoted in Poverty and Development into the 21st Century, 2000

of children will die before their fifth birthday, mainly from diseases related to their diet and living conditions. Parents may therefore have many children to ensure that at least some will survive beyond infancy. Their survival is important because many poorer countries have no social security system; instead parents rely on their children for support as they grow older. Children are also important in developing countries where much work is still labour-intensive. Here children may be vital members of the labour force, just as they were in pre-industrial Europe and North America.

FACT

By the age of twelve, children in developing countries may contribute as much to household income and survival as their parents.

Families in many developing countries may choose to have many children because of their value as contributors to the household income. This eleven-year-old boy and nine-year-old girl make bricks with their family near Lima, the capital of Peru.

Village health programmes, such as this one in Burkina Faso, are helping to improve child survival rates.

Children's work is particularly important in rural parts of developing countries. Children as young as seven can be found digging in the fields, scaring birds from crops or herding cattle. Alternatively, they may be cooking, cleaning or looking after younger children in the home while their parents work. In such circumstances parents who have many children may be 'wealthier' than those with fewer because their children contribute more towards the household than they take out. In this way, children can help their parents to escape poverty and having many children may even be a status symbol.

The importance of education and health

However, as more children survive infancy, having many children is becoming a burden for many poor people. Land and resources are scarcer and machines are being used to do much of the work. The opportunities to have large families are decreasing; instead they are forced to survive on what they have. In these situations many families, especially women, want fewer children. But their poverty means they often lack education and access to family planning facilities. This makes it harder for them to make decisions about the number of children they have, because they have no

VIEWPOINTS

'If there is a tendency of families to raise expenditure on children as their income rises, this by itself causes the price of children to rise and should reduce the number of children.'
Yoram Ben Porath, quoted in The Earthscan Reader in Population and Development, 1998

'Can you imagine parents sitting at the kitchen table with a calculator, working out the future economic benefits of their children?'
Tom Hewitt and Ines Smyth, quoted in Poverty and Development into the 21st Century, 2000

knowledge of, or access to, contraception. In better-educated and wealthier nations around 75 per cent of couples use some form of contraception. But in poorer countries, with high fertility and population growth rates, contraceptives are used by less than 20 per cent of couples.

Overcoming poverty

Most governments now agree that reducing poverty by improving health and education will automatically help control population. People tend to choose to have fewer children when they are educated, healthy and earn enough to afford access to services that ensure their family's survival. Many of the poorest governments, however, find it hard to fund such improvements due to large debts. Jamaica, for example, has debts equivalent to almost 98 per cent of its income, while Guyana and Mozambique owe more than twice as much as they currently earn. Some campaigners believe these debts should be written off to allow the poorest countries to invest in basic health and education to help them overcome poverty. This would in turn help to reduce their population growth.

FACT

It costs an average of more than £50,000 to feed, clothe and educate a child up to the age of adulthood (18) in the UK.

DEBATE

Think about the number of children in your immediate family. How do you think having more or fewer children would affect your family? Why would this be? How might your views change if you lived in an African or Indian village?

Reducing debts could benefit health and education programmes in developing regions.

POPULATION MOVEMENTS

VIEWPOINTS

'We want this to be a free country for everyone, but at the same time we think only certain people should be entitled to American privileges.'
Daphne Spain, author of Population Reference Bureau Reports on America

'The projected population decline and population ageing will have profound and far-reaching consequences forcing governments to reassess many established economic, social and political policies and programmes, including those relating to international migration'
United Nations Population Division

A world on the move

Today, more than ever, we live in a world that is on the move. In a few hours modern aircraft allow us to travel thousands of kilometres, distances that 100 years ago would have taken several weeks. We might make such journeys to visit family or go on holiday, but we normally return to where we started soon afterwards. For millions of people, though, movement is essential to find work or survive in difficult environments. And for some, movement may be necessary to escape conflict or because their well-being is threatened. These movements may be for long periods or even permanent.

Migration and population growth

Historically, people have moved between countries or areas to take advantage of new-found natural resources or to reduce the pressure on resources in heavily populated areas. We call such movements 'migration' and there are two main types: 'emigration' is when people (emigrants) leave an area for somewhere else; whereas 'immigration' is when people (immigrants) arrive in a country or area from elsewhere. You have probably seen immigration signs for new arrivals if you have travelled through an international air or sea port.

During the early part of the last century many British people emigrated to British colonies such as Australia, Kenya and India. And in the 1950s many Caribbean and South Asian people migrated to Britain to fill the demand for workers after the Second World War. More recently, one of the biggest migrations has taken place in Indonesia. Starting in 1984, the Indonesian government has moved millions of its people from the overcrowded islands of Java and Bali to the less populated islands of Sumatra, Irian Jaya and Kalimantan.

Such movements can have a major impact on a country's population. Between 1970 and 1995, for example, immigrants to the USA added 16.7 million to its population (accounting for about 6.3 per cent of the total population in 1995). Meanwhile in neighbouring Mexico, large-scale emigration meant there were 6 million fewer people over the same period (equivalent to 6.4 per cent of its 1995 population).

FACT

11 per cent of South Africa's population are white descendants of immigrants who came from the Netherlands and Britain during the late nineteenth century following the discovery of diamonds and gold.

London, UK, is today a multicultural city due to population movements over time. These Bengali youths show a newspaper in their language.

Moving to survive

Some people move great distances as part of their normal lives. These people are often known as nomads and they usually move with livestock such

as cattle, sheep, goats or camels. The animals are used to provide hides, meat and milk for consumption or for trade. One such group is the Tuareg people who live in the Sahara Desert in West Africa. Because of the low rainfall in this region the Tuareg may travel up to 1,600 km a year in search of grazing lands and water for their animals. They travel in small groups, moving frequently to allow the vegetation time to recover and so stay within the carrying capacity of their environment. Population growth in the region threatens the Tuareg because their traditional grazing lands are increasingly being used by more permanent settlers. The Tuareg and other nomadic groups have also encountered problems because their movements cross international borders that did not previously exist.

The Tuareg of West Africa have to travel great distances in order to survive.

FACT

Movement is so important to the San people of the Kalahari Desert in southern Africa that they will only have a second child once their first is strong enough to walk and carry its own belongings.

Employment movements

People often move to find employment or because countries are short of a particular type of worker. During 2000, for example, the British and Irish governments recruited nurses from the Philippines to fill staff shortages in their health services.

A well-known employment movement is that of Mexicans crossing into the USA in search of work. Mexico's average annual income is just US$3,700 per person but many Mexicans earn less than half this amount. For them the USA, with average incomes of almost US$30,000, offers hope of higher wages and a better future for their families. The attraction is so great that over 4,000 Mexicans attempt to cross illegally into the USA every night. The real figure is undoubtedly higher as those counted are only the ones who are caught and returned by US border patrols. Yet many see the risk as worthwhile, and Mexico receives an estimated US$6 billion per year sent back from Mexicans in the USA to support families left behind. This makes workers who have emigrated to the USA Mexico's third largest source of foreign income after tourism and oil.

Many businesses in the USA tolerate this illegal movement because Mexicans will work for longer hours and lower wages than US citizens. In fact their labour is so important that a 'guest-worker scheme' may be introduced, giving them permission to work in the USA for short periods.

VIEWPOINT

'We were frightened before we came across because breaking the law was against our culture and we were all crying because we had been told that they [the Border Patrol] were very mean.'
José, an illegal Mexican immigrant, quoted in the Guardian

A Mexican youth is caught, by a US border patrol, illegally trying to cross into the USA in search of work.

Refugees

In 2000 the world had around 23 million officially registered refugees, and this number is expected to increase in the future. These are people who have been forced to leave their own country because their lives are in real danger. The danger often comes from civil wars, such as the ongoing conflicts in the Sudan or Afghanistan, both of which have caused millions of refugees to flee to safety in neighbouring countries. Millions more remain trapped in war-torn countries where they are unable to receive the help that refugees might

Refugees, like these Kosovans at a camp on the Kosovar-Macedonian border, are becoming more numerous globally as a result of conflicts and environmental pressure.

get from the international community. These are known as 'internally displaced' refugees. They currently number around 30 million, with most living in Africa (16 million), Asia (7 million) and Europe (5 million).

War is not the only cause of refugees. Environmental deterioration is increasingly forcing people to leave their land when it can no longer meet their basic needs. There are already an estimated 10 million environmental refugees worldwide, with a possible 50 million more expected by 2050 due to deforestation, desertification and global warming. Development projects, such as the Three Gorges Dam on the Yangtze River in China, can also displace people. When completed in 2009 the dam's reservoir is expected to flood eighteen cities and 32,000 hectares of farmland, leaving over 1.2 million people in need of resettlement.

Action and resistance

Developed nations are under pressure to assist refugees and economic migrants, but local residents often resist such actions. In US border towns some residents describe Mexican economic migrants as 'invaders'. Some have even suggested that the US army should send tanks and troops to stop them. And in the UK port of Dover in 2000 there were some violent clashes between refugees and local unemployed youths. The youths were angry that the British government appeared to be helping refugees more than its own citizens. These tensions are expected to increase as population movements become more widespread in the future.

VIEWPOINT

'You cannot achieve any objective when the rural people have been displaced as refugees or they lack peace of mind and security to plant and cultivate their land.'
General Olusegun Obasanjo, former Nigerian president

FACT

The number of people forced to leave their homes because of war, natural disasters and famines increased from about 2.5 million in 1975 to around 15 million in 1995.

DEBATE

Why do you think some people are opposed to immigrants arriving in their community? How would it make you feel to be treated in this way when you might be there out of need rather than choice?

CONTROLLING POPULATION GROWTH

VIEWPOINT

'In Latin America and in Asia – the continent on which most human beings live – access to contraception has helped fertility rates to fall by half in little more than a generation'
Population Action International. 'People in the Balance'. 2000

Should we control population growth?

We began this book by asking whether there was a need to control population growth and you may have already decided that something should be done. However it is not as simple as just making a decision because people have rights, including the right to decide how many children they have. So how can population growth be managed without depriving people of their basic human rights?

Freedom of choice

In 1994 population experts and government officials from 175 countries met in Cairo, Egypt, for the third International Conference on Population and Development (ICPD). This meeting was different from previous meetings (Bucharest 1974 and Mexico City 1984) because it rejected earlier ideas about controlling population directly. Instead it was agreed that the best way to manage future population growth was to support people in choosing the number of children they had. The role of women in making these decisions was recognized as particularly important. Many women, especially those living in developing countries, would like to have fewer children and longer gaps between each birth. At present there are an estimated 80 million unwanted pregnancies every year, which is more than the 78 million per year currently being added to global population. A further 120-150 million women would like to plan the spacing of their pregnancies more accurately to protect both their own health and that of their children.

The focus of population policies today then, is how to help women and their partners make choices that will help them avoid unwanted or frequent pregnancies. At the ICPD in 1994 experts suggested three main ways of achieving this: improved access to contraceptives, a reduction in child mortality (death) rates, and the promotion of women's rights to reproductive healthcare.

FACT

Contraceptive use in Africa increased from 3 per cent in 1986 to 12 per cent in 2000. However, the continent still has by far the world's lowest use of contraceptives.

Improved access to contraceptives

Contraceptives, such as condoms or the female pill, are used by around 75 per cent of couples in countries like France, Denmark, the USA and the UK. They help prevent unwanted pregnancies and allow women to control when and how many children they have.

Family planning, as promoted by this Nigerian poster, helps couples choose how many children they have and when they have them.

Poor access to contraceptives in developing countries means family sizes are often very large. This family in Uganda has seventeen members.

In many poorer countries contraception use is much lower, which means that couples have less control over the size of their family. For example in Uganda only 15 per cent of couples use contraceptives, while Sierra Leone has one of the lowest levels in the world at just 4 per cent. Even when contraceptives are available in these countries some people are suspicious because they do not know enough about them. In Uganda some women believe that taking the contraceptive pill means you can never have children again. Misinformation problems like this can be solved through education programmes. These are often aimed at schoolchildren who will be the next generation of parents.

Contraceptives can be expensive, but many governments encourage greater use by subsidizing them or providing them free of charge. This is especially true of condoms, which are not only a reliable form of contraception but also vital in controlling Sexually Transmitted Diseases (STDs) and, more recently, the spread of the Human Immuno-Deficiency Virus (HIV) that causes AIDS (see page 56). Not everyone agrees on using contraceptives to control pregnancies. The Pope, who is the head of the Roman Catholic Church, opposes the use of contraceptives, a belief that may influence around 921 million Catholics worldwide. Not all Catholics follow the Pope's dictates however. In Italy, where almost 82 per cent of the population are Catholics, contraceptives are used by 78 per cent of couples and the population is expected to decrease by 28 per cent by 2050.

VIEWPOINT

'We clearly have a long way to go. But population programs have made a difference. Without them, the world's population would be much larger. Many societies would be less developed economically and socially.'
Kofi Annan, United Nations General Secretary

Reducing child mortality

Better basic healthcare, the education of women and girls, and improvements in living conditions have all been shown to reduce child mortality – one of the biggest influences on population growth rates. Child immunization programmes, such as the 'Kick Polio Out of Africa' campaign, aim to reduce mortality from preventable diseases including polio, measles and tuberculosis. Sub-Saharan Africa is the least immunized region: 33 per cent of one-year-olds are not being immunized against tuberculosis (TB) and 47 per cent are not protected against measles.

Education is the most effective way to reduce child mortality. Teaching people to keep their living environments clean and to wash their hands after going to the toilet can reduce disease dramatically.

Year	Reported global polio cases
1980	52,552
1985	38,637
1990	23,484
1995	7,035
2000	3,600

Source: Vital Signs 1999/2000

FACT

In Asia, Africa and Latin America women with seven or more years of schooling have 2–3 children less than women with three years of schooling or less.

Basic hygiene, such as this Kenyan girl washing her hands before she eats, has helped to reduce child mortality significantly.

FACT

Due to gender imbalances in China an estimated 111 million men will struggle to find wives because of a shortage of women.

FACT

In Tamil Nadu in India an estimated 3,000 baby girls were killed at birth between 1994 and 1997 due to the cultural preference for sons.

Education about contraceptives and their use helps to overcome suspicions and fears.

Mosquitoes, for example, breed in still pools of water; so making sure that there is no standing water around the home can reduce the number of mosquitoes and therefore the chances of catching malaria from their bites. The education of girls and women is especially important as they normally care for the young children who are most vulnerable. They will also pass their knowledge on to their own children.

Women's reproductive rights

Women are treated differently from men in most societies, and these differences can be extreme in much of the developing world. In South Asia, boys are more likely to be educated than girls and women's average incomes are about a third those of men. Women often have less access to information and health services to control the number of children they have. Improving their access to such services is a major priority in helping to slow population growth. After all, as we saw earlier, there are more unwanted pregnancies each year than the actual increase in population. These could

独生证 妈妈只生我一个

MAMAZHISHENGWOYI

A poster promoting China's controversial 'one child policy'.

perhaps be avoided if women had better access to facilities and information in the first place. However, women should also receive help if they want more children or if they face difficulties in having any at all. This is a growing problem in developed countries where women are choosing to have children later in life.

Other population policies

In 1979 China introduced a strict 'one child policy', under which married couples had to apply to the state for permission to have a child. They would be guaranteed free education for the child, a state pension and various other family benefits. If they had a second child, however, they would lose these benefits and could be fined up to 15 per cent of their income or even lose their jobs. The cultural preference for boys means there is now a gender imbalance, with many millions less girls in China. Some couples who gave birth to a girl are even rumoured to have left them to die so that they could try again for a boy. Gender imbalances have also been identified in India and other South Asian countries, for similar reasons as in China.

VIEWPOINTS

'Women around the world would have preferred to delay or avoid about 25 to 40 per cent of all pregnancies that have taken place.'
Margaret Catley-Carlson, President of Population Council

'In many societies a young woman is still trapped within a web of traditional values which assign a very high value to child-bearing and almost none to anything else she can do. Her status depends on her success as a mother and on little else.'
United Nations Population Fund

DEBATE

It will probably be some time before you think about having your own children, but try to imagine how you would feel if someone tried to tell you how many children you could have. What do your feelings tell you about the difficulties governments face in trying to control population?

HOW MANY PEOPLE?

VIEWPOINTS

'At the start of a new century it is more obvious than ever before that humanity needs to stabilize its numbers.'
Kofi Annan, United Nations General Secretary, 2000

'Arresting global population growth should be second in importance only to avoiding nuclear war on humanity's agenda.'
The Club of Earth, 1988, in The Population Explosion 1990

FACT

8,500 young people and children around the world are infected with HIV every day.

The numbers game

As you can see, population is a complicated issue that raises many questions. And there is still an important debate as to whether or not the world is overcrowded. Resources such as oil are running low, millions of people are suffering hunger and poverty, and it looks certain that our activities are changing our climate. But new technologies allow people to live healthier and longer lives than ever before. The discovery of new materials and industrial processes allows us to use resources more efficiently and the level of concern for the environment is increasing. But the question remains: how many people can the world support?

The United Nations Population Division has the job of predicting world population. In recent years they have reduced their estimates significantly. In 1992 they predicted a population of 11.6 billion by 2150, but this has now been reduced to 9.75 billion. Lower estimates show that population could increase to only 6.4 billion by 2150, while some even suggest a reduction to 3.6 billion, though this is very unlikely. Predicting numbers is difficult because there are so many factors that can affect population. One factor that affects current predictions more than any other is the impact of HIV/AIDS.

HIV/AIDS and population

During the 1980s HIV emerged as a new disease. Scientists did not know where it came from or fully understand how people became infected. They did know that there was no cure and that it could kill

otherwise healthy people very quickly. We now know that HIV is spread by having unprotected sex or sharing needles with, or receiving blood from, an infected person. There is still no cure, but special drugs allow people suffering HIV to live a normal life for longer. These drugs are very expensive, and governments and individuals in most developing countries cannot afford them. They argue that the companies making them in Europe and North America should reduce their price in order to increase the life expectancy of millions of sufferers and help prevent mothers passing the disease on to their unborn babies.

This cemetery in Lusaka, Zambia, struggles to keep pace with the burial of AIDS victims who are dying in ever-increasing numbers.

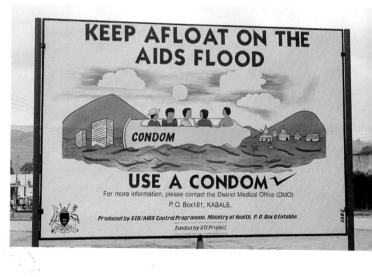

AIDS awareness posters have helped reduce infection rates in Uganda.

VIEWPOINTS

'It is obscene that 98–99 per cent of those in greatest need are denied access to [HIV] drugs because they cannot afford them.'
Nathan Ford, Medecins San Frontières

'We are a drug company and we do need to make a profit. A drug takes 15 years from concept to market. Drug companies need to recoup their investment and research.'
Jennifer Perry, pharmaceutical company

But companies have spent millions of dollars developing drugs and they say they cannot lower prices if they are to continue searching for a cure for HIV. While arguments over the cost of the drugs continue, millions of people are dying because of HIV. The worst affected area is sub-Saharan Africa. In Botswana and Zimbabwe, more than one in four people over fifteen years of age is infected with HIV. This has caused life expectancy to fall by almost twenty years in Zimbabwe, from sixty-three in 1990-95 to just forty-four for a child born in 1995-2000. If this continues, Zimbabwe's population will be 19 per cent smaller by 2015 than it would have been without HIV. (This means 3.2 million fewer people.) The impact of HIV is so great that population growth rates may halve by 2015 for some countries.

A balancing act

HIV/AIDS, improved healthcare and education, and individuals choosing to have fewer children may all be slowing population growth, but what effect do these factors really have? The actual number of people in the world is still growing by about 78 million per year. More significantly, each new person has a bigger impact on the planet than their parents or grandparents, especially those born

FACT

AIDS kills more people than war. In Africa, in 1998, 200,000 people were killed in conflicts, but AIDS killed 2 million.

Ecologically friendly homes, like this one in Denmark, help to reduce human impact on the planet.

in developed nations. So it's as much a question of how we live, as of how many of us there are. The solution could lie in creating a balance between human needs and the ability of the planet to meet those needs, both now and in the future. This idea is known as sustainable development. Consuming less, recycling more and using renewable resources are all ways in which this might be achieved.

Each of us can play a part by thinking about our own lives. When your children reach your age, the world population will probably be approaching 8.5 billion people. What will their world be like and what about the world of their children – your grandchildren? If we agree that population and its impact on the planet is best managed by individual choice, then it is up to us to make those choices now.

VIEWPOINT

'In our every deliberation, we must consider the impact of our decisions on the next seven generations'
Great Law of the Iroquois Confederacy

The world this Indian boy's grandchildren will grow up in will depend largely on decisions made by his generation – including you!

DEBATE

Thinking about what you have learned about population and its impact on our planet, are you more of an optimist or a pessimist about future population growth? What reasons would you give to support your view?

GLOSSARY

birth rate the number of babies born per 1,000 people in a particular year.

carrying capacity the total population that an ecosystem can support without being damaged.

consumer lifestyle way of life in which the vast majority of people's needs and wants are met through the purchase of goods and services, especially those that are mass-produced.

contraception the planned prevention of unwanted pregnancy (sometimes called birth control).

deforestation the removal of trees, shrubs and forest vegetation. This can be natural (due to forest fires, typhoons, etc.) or a result of human action (logging, ranching, construction, land clearance, etc.).

demographer someone who studies populations and changes in population – the science of demography.

desertification a condition whereby soils lose their fertility. This can be due to topsoil loss because of erosion or the removal of vegetation, or as a result of intensive agriculture practices that fail to give soils time to recover between growth cycles.

developed countries generally wealthier countries of the world, including those of Europe and North America, Japan and Australia and New Zealand. People living there usually benefit from good health and education, and work in a variety of service and high-technology industries.

developing countries generally poorer countries of the world, sometimes called the Third World and including most of Africa, Asia, Latin America and Oceania. People living there often suffer poor health and education and work in agriculture and lower-technology industries.

ecosystem the contents of an environment, including all the plants and animals that live there. This could be a garden pond, a forest or the whole of planet earth.

emigration a movement of people away from an area. Such people are known as emigrants.

emissions waste products (normally gases and solid particles) released into the atmosphere. These include car exhaust fumes and the wastes from chimneys at power stations and factories.

family planning a range of services and information that allow couples (and especially women) to choose the number of children they have and when they have them.

fertility the ability to reproduce/have children. The fertility rate is the number of children that an average woman in a particular society would be expected to have during her reproductive lifetime.

food aid the giving of food to meet shortages in supply and avoid hunger and starvation. Food aid can also be given to assist poor communities, even when there is no immediate threat of starvation.

fossil fuels energy sources such as coal, oil and gas formed millions of years ago by the fossilized remains of plants and animals.

global warming the gradual warming of the earth's atmosphere as a result of carbon dioxide emissions and other greenhouse gases trapping heat.

Green Revolution the introduction of High Yield Varieties (HYVs) of wheat, rice and other cereal crops that began in the 1960s.

HIV/AIDS Human Immunodeficiency Virus (HIV) is a deadly virus spread by unprotected sex or contaminated needles or blood supplies. It can develop into Acquired Immuno-Deficiency Syndrome (AIDS), which is fatal. Expensive drugs can keep people alive, but there is no cure.

HYV crops High Yield Variety (HYV) crops are specially bred in laboratory conditions to produce higher yields than existing varieties. They were the main ingredient of the Green Revolution.

immigration a movement of people into an area. Such people are known as immigrants.

immunization the giving of medicines (normally as an injection) to protect against the risk of catching diseases such as polio, measles and typhoid.

Industrial Revolution the period in the late eighteenth century and early nineteenth century (150-250 years ago) in Europe when new machinery and the use of fossil fuels to generate energy led to the start of modern industry and dramatic changes in the way people lived.

life expectancy the average expected lifetime of a person born in any particular year – measured in years.

malnutrition deficiency in the nutrients that are essential for the development of the body and for its maintenance in adulthood.

mega-cities cities that have a population of more than 10 million.

migration the movement of people (migrants). Migration can be temporary or permanent and includes movement over short distances (e.g. from country to town) or large distances (e.g. from one continent to another).

mortality rate the number of people who die per 1,000 people in a particular year.

nomads people who move from place to place as part of their daily life. Normally rural people, moving with their livestock to find water and pasture.

obesity the condition of being clinically overweight.

ozone depletion the disappearance of the ozone layer – a layer of gas in the atmosphere that protects the earth from the sun's harmful ultraviolet rays.

population the total number of people living in a particular area such as a town, province or country.

population density the number of people living in any particular area, normally calculated as people per square kilometre.

population growth rate the speed at which a population is growing. It is normally expressed as a percentage figure.

population momentum the continued growth of a population due to a large number of young people in the population who are entering their main reproductive stage of life.

refugees people who are forced to move from their normal place of residence due to circumstances that threaten their well-being (e.g. conflict or drought).

resources the materials and energy used in making products or providing services. Resources can be thought of as ingredients.

sewage waste carried by sewers for treatment or disposal. Sewage normally includes human wastes and waste water, but can include chemicals from homes, offices and factories.

sustainable development development that meets the requirements of today's generation without damaging the ability of future generations to meet their needs.

urbanization the process of a region or country's population increasingly living in urban areas (towns or cities).

BOOKS TO READ

Living for the Future: World Population
Nance Fyson
(Franklin Watts, 2000)

Living for the Future: Homes and Cities
Sally Morgan
(Franklin Watts, 1997)

USEFUL ADDRESSES

http://www.prb.org
The Population Reference Bureau is one of the best sites for information about population issues, with regularly updated news stories and features. Not specifically aimed at young people, but clearly designed and easy to navigate.

http://www.popnet.org
This site has links to hundreds of other sites at both a global and local level for countries around the world. Useful for those who want to research this topic in greater detail.

http://www.un.org/esa/population/unpop.htm
The homepage of the United Nations Population Division, containing a wide range of regularly updated information. Links to the interactive population centre are particularly useful for learning more, including the day of 6 billion page with a clock showing real-time population growth.

http://www.enviroliteracy.org
A website that is searchable by topic, including population as a key category. Provides its own information files, with hotlinks to further sources.

http://www.census.gov/ipc/www/world.html
A very useful site for finding up-to-the minute population data for almost any country of your choosing. The dynamic population pyramids are especially interesting as they show how the structure of a population changes over time.

http://www.populationconnection.org/education/
The education page for the organization Population Connection (formerly known as Zero Population Growth), which is concerned about population growth and the impact it has on the planet.

INDEX

INDEX